HOW TO STOP YOUR *Marriage* FROM BREAKING UP

Avoiding Ten Major Relationship Killers

Published by

T P PUBLICATIONS
4 Pegamoid Road.
Edmonton. London.
N18 2NG.

ISBN 978-1-874332-58-9

Author's Website & Blog Page
http://www.rocksolidmarriages.com

CONTENT

Introduction 5

1. The Urge To Control Or Change Your Spouse 7

2. The Need To Be Right, At Any Cost 11

3. The Temptation To Retaliate And Not Forgive 15

4. The Urge To Criticise Far More Than You Encourage 19

5. The Temptation to Shame and Insult Your Spouse 23

6. The Tendency to be Highly Defensive 27

7. The Refusal To Communicate How You Are Feeling 31

8. The Temptation To Respond To Issues In An Unbridled Manner 35

9. The Habit Of Digging Up Past Hurts And Wounds 39

10. The Habit of Stone–walling 43

Final Word 48

INTRODUCTION

"Do your part to live in peace with everyone, as much as possible."
(Romans 12:18.)

As you embark on the journey to build a great marriage or relationship, you must be careful not to tear down—with your own hands, so to speak—what you are trying to build.

It is one thing to protect your marriage from outside forces, over which you have little control; but it is quite another thing to protect your marriage from 'inward' mindsets, attitude and behaviour, over which you do have substantial control.

So, I want to highlight ten relationship killers or 'inner enemies' of a strong marriage relationship. I call them 'inner' enemies because they come from deep within us and are products of our thought patterns, our fears, our values, our insecurities, and even our upbringing.

I call them 'relationship killers' because they strangle our relationships of emotional oxygen and deprive us of the beautiful life we were destined to enjoy.

CHAPTER 1

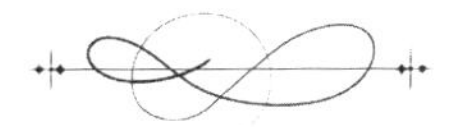

The Urge To Control Or Change Your Spouse

Changing what you do is the key to changing what others do: since they often take their cue from you – Eagle Prince.

Human beings were never created to be controlled. We were created to rule, govern and display dominion over the works of God's Hands. We were put on this earth to grow.

That's why two-year-old kids start to rebel against all forms of control, as soon as they start thinking for themselves. As we grow older, we get even more spiteful and aggressive towards any hint of domination. Again, that's why controlling relationships are never healthy, and never work.

God intentionally created us to be different and to prefer different things, so that when we come together in marriage, there would be variety. God designed us to function like the ivory and ebony keys on a grand piano. The keys are very different in colour and tune, but together they produce angelic music at the hands of a Master Pianist.

Therefore, one way to grow a great relationship with someone very different from you is to get excited about their uniqueness (who they are and what they like) and decide to be happy for them and for the variety they bring to the relationship.

For instance, my wife loves romantic and tender family friendly films. I like action-packed, car-chasing, building-exploding, machine-gun blasting blockbusters. Happily, I learnt early in my marriage that I was not going to change my wife's film preference and she was not going to change mine.

So, instead of trying to change each other or allowing our difference to separate us, we learnt to be selfless. I learnt to enjoy (what I called) ‘girly’ films with my wife – so that we could be together; and she learnt to share in my adrenalin producing movies.

Controlling your spouse or trying to force him/her to do what you want is demeaning and humiliating. Your spouse may put up with it for a while to keep the peace, but lasting joy and satisfaction will evaporate under the scotching heat of ‘control’.

Kill the urge to change or control your spouse before it kills your marriage. Except your spouse is doing something morally wrong or abusive to you, you have no right to try to change him/her. Just because something is different doesn’t make it wrong.

Your relationship will blossom and flourish when your goal is to please and pleasure your partner. But to do that you must understand that being controlling is always counter-productive; and being selfless is always better.

“Do nothing from selfishness or pride, but in humility count others better than yourself. (Philippians 2:3.)

An ordinary journey becomes extraordinary, when it is taken with the right person – Eagle Prince.

CHAPTER 2

The Need To Be Right, At Any Cost

The need to be 'right' at any cost is the Achilles heel of opinionated people
– Eagle Prince

Your marriage will be toxic if you are always out to win the argument or be 'right'. That's because you will continue to bruise your partner's ego by insisting that he/she is always wrong. After all, if you are always 'right', your spouse, of necessity, must always be wrong.

If you keep doing this, what your spouse is constantly hearing is, "You are dumb", "You are unintelligent", "You are thick", and "We are not in the same league". Even if you are actually wiser or more intelligent, you must go out of your way to help your spouse see that he/she is not totally clueless or without a brain. Anything less is prideful and deadly to the marriage.

"Pride ends in humiliation, while humility brings honour."

(Proverbs 29:23.)

In fact, if you really love your spouse, you would be looking for ways to elevate him/her, because your spouse, in the final analysis, is a reflection on you. Yes, your spouse is a reflection on you. After all, you chose, courted, and married this 'dumb' person.

If you keep projecting stupidity onto your spouse, you must be 'stupid' too for marrying him/her. Were you blind? Were you gagged? Did someone hold a gun to your head? I don't think so. My point is that your spouse is not what you are making him/her out to be.

Give your spouse's ideas a chance to succeed. Give him/her credit for some of the things they bring to the table. Don't sabotage good ideas to score points. Don't shut your spouse up because you are not in agreement with his/her ideas or because you feel yours are better. Don't shoot your spouse down because you always want to be 'right'.

Learn to be charitable enough to boost your spouse's confidence; by adopting his/her ideas and making them work. You can't do this if you are always right, or if you take all the decisions, or if you always insist on doing things your way.

Which is better: To be 'right' and miserable or to share in decision-making and be united? An unhappy marriage and an insecure spouse is too great a price to pay for being 'right'. If being 'right' is really right, it should lead to good things. If it's not, it's not really right.

So, kill the need to be right at any cost and you'd be surprised at how right your spouse can be if you put the effort you put into being 'right', into making sure that your spouse is secure and right too. If you understand the marriage vows you took, you will understand that it is your duty to build your spouse up, not to tear him/her down.

(To understand your marriage vows better, you may want to read another one of my books on Amazon.com, Smashword.com or iBooks titled: **Understand Your Marriage Vows**–What the Marriage Vows Mean and How to Honour Them.

If your reason is right, but your attitude or actions are wrong, the outcome will still be negative – Eagle Prince.

CHAPTER 3

The Temptation To Retaliate And Not Forgive

Without forgiveness life is governed by an endless cycle of resentment and retaliation – Roberto Assagioli

Retaliation is a very human trait. When we've been offended, we feel bad and tell ourselves that we would feel better once our offender has been made to feel the pain we felt. The truth, though, is that we often feel worst for retaliating, because it seldom takes away our pain. Instead, it produces more hurt and more reprisal.

But, especially in marriage, retaliation never really mends or heals anything. What heals is forgiveness. What repairs the pain is learning to transform our negative energy into a positive one. What mends the fracture in our relationship is love and kindness.

That only happens when you value and exercise forgiveness. Forgiveness is the antidote for retaliation. God promises to level the score if we leave every offence committed against us in His capable hands. That's what we read in Paul's Epistle to the Roman Christians:

Dear friends, never avenge yourself. Leave that to God. For it is written, "I will take vengeance; I will repay those who deserve it," says the Lord.

I know that it's not easy to forgive on your own. But if you ask for God's help, He will empower you to see things in perspective. He will help you see how you also offend your spouse – some times knowingly, and some times unknowingly.

He will show you how self-defeating unresolved anger, unforgiveness and retaliation are to your health and your peace of mind. He will remind you that you offend Him daily (with things that you should do, but you don't; and things that you shouldn't do, but you do), and expect Him to forgive you.

Well, He expects you to extend that same grace and forgiveness to your spouse. After all, he/she is only human. Learn to forgive and release your spouse into the hands of God, and never allow your actions to be controlled by your emotions.

Retaliation never accomplishes anything good anyway – only forgiveness does.

Peter said to Him, "Lord, how often shall my brother sin against me, and I forgive him? Up to seven times?" Jesus said to him, "I do not say to you, up to seven times, but up to seventy times seven." (Matthew 18:21-22.)

One last word here: If your spouse's offences are intentional and continuous, or boarding on serious abuse, go and get advice from a marriage counsellor or a respected minister.

I don't think God wants you to suffer in silence; and I don't think forgiveness should prevent you from seeking help if things are getting out of hand. The crucial thing is that you are not looking to retaliate, because retaliation hurts you as well. And sometimes, it even hurts you more than it hurts the person it was aimed at.

CHAPTER 4

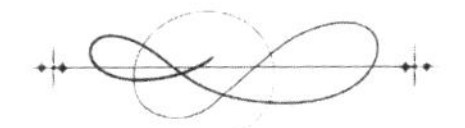

The Urge To Criticise Far More Than You Encourage

One choice word of encouragement will do more good than a thousand cruel words of criticism – Eagle Prince.

Nobody wants to be criticised, belittled or attacked all the time. Yet we thoughtlessly do it to the people we say we love the most. It is wise to remember that everyone has something going on in their life for which they can be praised or encouraged.

In fact, encouragement is what helps us grow and improve. Constant criticism only makes us want to give up, as we feel there is nothing we can do to appease our critic. I'm sure you know the feeling. You do your best, you burst your guts, but your best is not good enough for Mr or Mrs Never Satisfied.

My point is that your spouse needs to hear your encouraging words more than your critical and negative ones. I am not for a minute suggesting that you should always ignore or overlook issues that need to be dealt with, but that you should realise the damage that constant rebuke, criticism and condemnation is having on your relationship.

If you have complaint that you need to bring to your spouse, by all means address it. But understand that a complaint carefully addresses the issue, while criticism carelessly blames the person.

Resist the temptation to start criticising your spouse when you are trying to bring his/her attention to a complaint. Resist the urge to dish out negative and critical comments every time you are not happy with something; because the spirit behind this attitude is often worst than the thing that you are trying to correct.

I feel I need to repeat what I've just stated. The ugly judgmental spirit behind negative criticism is often worst than the thing that you are trying to correct. In other words, you can't change a negative situation with a negative spirit or attitude.

Even when your spouse is doing something you don't like, you don't have to verbalise it in a critical way again and again. If you've said it a couple of times before, your spouse already knows how you feel about the issue.

The trick is to give your spouse time to come to the conclusion you've come to, and want the change too. That's why patience is crucial. Self-leadership always works better than trying to get your spouse to do something he/she is not emotionally committed to yet.

If, in the mean time, you would spend your energy in praising and encouraging your spouse for the things he/she gets right, two things will happen in your marriage before long:

You'd start to see less of the things that used to bug you so much about your spouse. Why? Because your attention and energy are now positively focused.

Your spouse would start to put more effort into doing the things that attract your approval.

Why? Because your spouse (like the rest of us) values the praise and encouragement she/he gets from loved ones.

Do you find yourself constantly criticising and disapproving of your spouse's behaviour or choices? If you do, you must take steps to stop it, because it is a marriage killer. Criticising your spouse will stifle communication; it will smother openness; it will provoke bitterness; and it will breed destructive conflict.

In the end, a rock solid marriage can only be built on a rock solid foundation of acceptance, encouragement and positive affirmations.

Don't use foul or abusive language. Let everything you say be good and helpful, so that your words will be an encouragement to those who hear them. (Ephesians 4:29.)

"So then, let us aim for peace and harmony... and try to build each other up." (Romans 14:19.)

CHAPTER 5

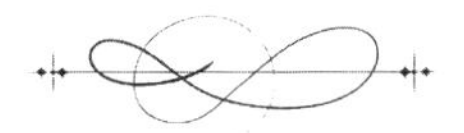

The Temptation to Shame and Insult your Spouse

Let no corrupt speech proceed out of your mouth, but such as is good for building up as the need may be, that it may give grace to those who hear. Let all bitterness, wrath, anger, outcry, and slander, be put away from you, with all malice. (Ephesians 4:29,31.)

Many of us grew up in an era when shaming and insulting were deployed as corrective tools. When I was growing up, it was foolishly believed that if you shamed or insulted someone enough they would be motivated to change their ways. But the results didn't bear out this belief.

For instance, the teachers we had back then would publicly call out our marks and grades for the whole class to hear. One teacher would say something like: “If you don’t want everyone to think that you are a ‘lazy bum’; you better work harder the next time I give you an assignment”. What she didn’t know was that being a ‘lazy bum’ was actually a badge of honour for some of the students.

The ‘shaming thing’ not only didn’t work for many of us, but it had the very opposite effect on some kids, because it made them popular amongst their peers. It gave them the attention they badly needed.

Insulting or shaming your spouse never works in a marriage either. It produces resentment, anger and a desire for revenge. Insulting and shaming is disrespectful and antagonistic. It is never motivates a person to change, except to become more negative and hateful towards you.

Let’s say you are having an argument with your spouse and you decide to remind him that he comes from a broken home or is behaving like his atrocious father. Do you think he would put his hands up in surrender and thank you for being so perceptive and right? No, no, no!

You have just shamed and insulted him, even if what you said was true. Nine out of ten times, he will fight back. Why? Because insults bring out the worst in us. Insults hurt us deeply. They shame us profoundly. Insults take a swipe at our identity and our self-worth. And, if that was not enough, insults make us feel severely demeaned, debased and devalued.

Don't call your spouse names. Don't compare him/her to some dysfunctional person. Don't insult his family, or abuse her siblings. Don't take a cheap swing at your partner's physical features; and don't swear at him/her either. In the final analysis, whatever you see in your partner is a reflection on you, because you chose him/her to be your partner – warts, bumps and all.

That's why you must never go down that path. It will damage your marriage in unimaginable ways. If you have done so in the past, I appeal to you to repent and ask for your spouse's forgiveness; and never do it again. I don't care how upset or angry you are, never insult or shame your spouse. What's the reason? Your spouse is the apple of God's eye and was made in the image of God!

Don't insult or shame your partner privately, and never ever do it publicly either.

So be kind to one another, tenderhearted, forgiving each other, just as God also in Christ forgave you.

(Ephesians 4:32.)

CHAPTER 6

The Tendency to be Highly Defensive

When people have something to hide, they become unusually defensive
– Eagle Prince.

Another major relationship killer is the tendency to always defend your position even when it is indefensible. For instance, your spouse asks you to get three or four items from the corner-shop on your way home from work. You promise to do so and you leave for work.

When you return that evening, your spouse asks you for the items. You forgot to get them. What do you do? Well, if you are mature, you apologise for forgetting and try to rectify the situation.

If, on the other hand, you are in the habit of being defensive, you would begin to blame events and people who have nothing to do with your forgetfulness.

"Why are you upset with me? After all, I was rushing home to be with you." you say defensively (and dishonestly).

"If you had written and list for me, I would have remembered to buy the stuff", you say defensively.

"Why don't you buy them yourself? After all, you know I always forget these kinds of errands." you say again defensively.

When you are defensive:

- **You lie to yourself and try to lie to others.**
- **You put up walls that isolate you from your spouse.**
- **You make the issue you are trying to resolve worse.**
- **You deflect blame or consequences away from yourself.**

- **You pass the buck to some imaginary person or thing.**
- **And, you invariably insult your spouse's intelligence.**

Your marriage will work better when you are open and humble enough to admit your fault; when you accept guilt or blame for things over which you are responsible; and when you don't justify your forgetfulness, failures or mistakes.

Realise that every time you get defensive, you are feeding your arrogance and starving yourself of humility. Every time you cover up your failings or justify mediocrity, you are banishing yourself to failure. Every time you deflect the blame onto someone else or something else, you are damaging your integrity in the eyes of your spouse or anyone listening.

The Bible puts it this way: "**Pride leads to destruction; humility leads to honour.**"

I like that. Your relationship will grow better when you are willing to be humble and vulnerable; when you stop pretending to be perfect; and when you start to take responsibility for your blunders.

People don't often want to be vulnerable because they falsely believe that they would be taken advantage of. That may happen occasionally; but from my experience, the majority of the time you would be respected for being humble enough to admit you are not Mr or Mrs Perfect.

The tendency to be defensive stops you and your partner from dealing with the real issues in your life and in your relationship. It puts up walls that can't be scaled. It brings up arguments that can't be resolved. It hinders your effort to move forward. And, it sabotages any attempt at mature conflict resolution.

So, if you really want to build a rock solid marriage, stop being defensive. Just say you are sorry!

If we claim that we've not missed the mark, we're only fooling ourselves. A claim like that is errant nonsense.
(1 John 1:8.)

CHAPTER 7

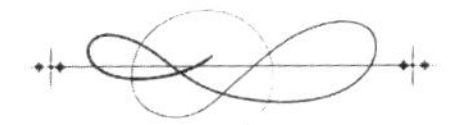

The Refusal To Communicate How You Are Feeling

When matters of the heart are brought out into the light, they lose their sting, their poison, and their power
– Eagle Prince.

Too many married people feel that the best way to deal with a challenge in their relationship is to shut their spouse out for a season and respond with the dreaded 'silent treatment'. That's when one or both parties refuse to speak to each other for as long as possible. They generally avoid each other and try to keep the sum total of their discussion to the 'read-my-mind' level.

But the refusal to communicate in marriage is a really dangerous strategy because, while it is often deployed to reduce the conflict at hand, it actually allows the conflict to grow into a monster.

The longer the silent treatment lasts, the more difficult it gets for the couple to talk about their pain and reconcile. As a result, lots of hurts get swept under the proverbial 'rug' and the hurts continue to fester in the dark recesses of their heart.

This destructive behaviour allows the couple to exaggerate the conflict, embellish the hurts, overstate the damage done, and make permanent decisions over temporary challenges. The enemy of your marriage just loves it when you don't communicate because it's a 'lose-lose' game for you and a 'win-win' game for him.

When you don't speak to your spouse after a relational setback, two things happen:

Firstly, you internalise and incubate toxic feelings that can eventually affect your health adversely.

Secondly, you deprive your spouse of an opportunity to apologise, explain, or understand how you are feeling.

If you have to retreat after a conflict to evaluate what happened so that your response can be measured and appropriate, that is good. But endeavour to keep the communication lines open as soon as humanly possible.

My wife and I decided earlier on in our marriage to sort out our arguments and quarrels before we went to bed. That means that we rarely went more than twenty-four hours before we sat down to talk. Well, that's precisely what God's Word instructs couples to do.

"And don't sin by letting anger gain control over you. Don't let the sun go down while you are still angry, for anger gives a mighty foothold to the Devil." (Ephesians 4:26-27.)

Sadly, too many couples give Satan a foothold into their lives because they wouldn't follow this divine injunction. Unfortunately, the results are devastating. I know, because I had an aunt who had a massive stroke because she allegedly kept too many painful experiences bottled up.

Irrespective of the type of temperament you have, you must learn to share what you are feeling with your spouse in a mature and positive way. If you don't, you risk hurting yourself by keeping alive the very thing that's hurting you. So, keep your lines of communication open, when you are tempted to shut them down.

Finally, if talking rationally to your spouse about your concerns is proving unproductive, find a helpful minister or marriage counsellor to talk to. Never keep the hurts and disappointments of your relationship hidden, because they are poisonous and toxic to your health and wellbeing.

When matters of the heart are brought out into the light, they lose their sting, their poison, and their power. When they are kept in the dark, they grow into unpredictable monsters that attempt to consume you.

CHAPTER 8

The Temptation To Respond To Issues In An Unbridled Manner

"When you talk, do not say harmful things, but say what people need—words that will help them become stronger. Then what you say will do good to those who listen to you." (Ephesians 4:29.)

When you are upset with your spouse, you'd be tempted to give him/her a piece of your mind. And it's usually the offensive piece. But I want to advice you not to act or speak so quickly, because words spoken in anger and actions taken in haste cannot be taken back easily.

Always ask yourself whether the things you want to say will make things better or worst. Will they harm or heal? Will they pacify or will they enrage your spouse? Ask yourself whether you'd regret saying it or whether you'd be pleased that you said it, when things get better between you.

In a troubled marriage, words are often more lethal than physical abuse because they go deeper. They hack at the soul; they the lacerate the ego; and they damage human dignity and self-esteem.

That's why the Bible instructs us to watch what we say.

"When you talk, do not say harmful things, but say what people need—words that will help them become stronger. Then what you say will do good to those who listen to you." (Ephesians 4:29.)

If you are a Believer, it is your duty to exercise self-control when you are under pressure. You are not an instinctive animal designed to respond to every challenge intuitively. God has given you the power of choice. You can choose how you respond to each challenge and conflict that confronts you.

When you are upset about something, you can decide not to let it change you. You can decide to pause and deal with the person who upset you lovingly. You can decide to go out for a walk and return with the wisdom of God to handle the situation maturely. In fact, you can do a thousand other things that wouldn't include an unbridled tantrum.

So, choose to respond to your spouse in love. Why? Because:

Love is patient and kind. Love is not jealous or boastful. It is not arrogant or rude or selfish or irritable or resentful. Love does not rejoice at wrong, but rejoices in the right. Love bears all things, believes all things, and endures all things. Love never fails.

(1 Corinthians 13:4-8.)

"... Above all things have fervent love for one another, for love will cover a multitude of sins." (1 Peter 4:8.)

In times of conflict and disagreement, choose to speak and act like a person who knows that you have the power of God in you. That's your prerogative! That's what it means to be a

Christ-follower. If you can't control your actions, who can?

The temptation to act in an unbridled and uncontrolled manner is a double-edged sword. It will hurt you as much, if not more, than it hurts your spouse.

If you find yourself getting so upset or angry that you blow your top, know that you are sinning against God and against your spouse. Repent and make amends; and watch God transform your marriage because of your commitment to do the right thing.

CHAPTER 9

The Habit Of Digging Up Past Hurts And Wounds

It's only prudent to focus on the rear view mirror, if you want to go backward, not if you want to go forward
– The Eagle Prince.

Another very common relationship killer is the addictive habit of digging up past hurts and issues that should have been forgiven and 'forgotten'. As believers, God expects us to really forgive people who hurt us – especially when they've asked to be forgiven.

"For if ye forgive men their trespasses, your heavenly Father will also forgive you. But if ye forgive not men their

trespasses, neither will your Father forgive your trespasses." (Matthew 6:14-15.)

Even if your partner hasn't yet asked to be forgiven, it is in your interest to do so.

Bringing up past hurts again and again is like peeling the scab off an old wound that's trying to heal. Instead of healing, the wound bleeds afresh and the healing process has to start from scratch again.

Digging up past offences only proves to your spouse that you are still holding on to these hurts. It also complicates the business of reconciliation, and will tend to make your spouse defensive and less apologetic.

That is because your partner feels that nothing he/she says is going to gain your forgiveness. Your spouse also feels that you are being unfair and vindictive.

When people dig up past hurts, it is usually to justify their anger or bad behaviour; or to shame their spouse into admitting failure. Either way, it is harmful and unfair to your spouse.

But you also get flooded when you dig up the hurts of your past. You relive past pain and disappointments. Your brain magnifies the challenges you are presently facing; so that it looks and feels worse than it actually is. Finally, you over-react and lose your sense of perspective.

If you must 'fight' with your partner, at least learn to 'fight' fair. Learn to deal with the issue at hand alone. Learn to keep the discussion simple, current and to the point.

If you've developed the habit of resurrecting past hurts and failures whenever you have a quarrel with you partner, stop it! It is hurting your relationship and giving you a bad reputation.

Now, I know that what I am encouraging you to do is not the easiest thing to do – especially when your spouse keeps doing the same things that caused conflict in the past. Nevertheless, if your partner has apologised or asked to be forgiven, you must decide to draw a line under the issue, bite your lips and never bring it up again.

If your spouse hasn't apologised, you may want to bring the issue up to let him/her know how you felt and how an apology would go a long way to rectifying the issue. But once your spouse has done his/her part, you must resolve to forgive and 'forget'.

I am convinced that if you would do this, your spouse would eventually realise the changes in you. And, because you are now sowing a different seed, you would start to reap a different harvest. God has a way of convicting and changing your spouse at the right time, when you have done what He expects you to do.

Now, that's all you can really ask for!

CHAPTER 10

The Habit of Stone-walling

When you disregard people, you insult them in silence – The Eagle Prince.

Another silent 'relationship killer' is the habit of stone-walling. In most normal conversations, the listener gives all kinds of cues to show that he/she is listening and engaging in what is being conveyed. Typically, the listener would nod intermittently, maintain eye contact or say something appropriate.

Stone-walling, on the other hand, is when the listener tunes out the speaker or sits impassively through the conversation like a stone wall. Stone-walling takes place any time you disengage and refuse to respond to your spouse's concerns or complaints.

Although this behaviour is often seen as a harmless way to avoid conflict or protect ourselves from quarrels, it is none-the-less a passive-aggressive behaviour. And, it can often hurt your partner and your marriage in deeper ways than an active aggressive behaviour can.

Stone-walling is passive-aggressive and dangerous because:

- ***It makes you look disengaged and uncaring.***
- ***Your spouse feels insulted by your behaviour.***
- ***It prevents the problem from being tackled or solved.***
- ***It points to you as the one avoiding your responsibilities.***
- ***Your spouse feels that everything he/she is said fell on deaf ears.***
- ***Your spouse stays in the dark as to how you are feeling or what you are thinking.***

I am sure that you don't like conflict. I don't know of anybody who does. But you must learn to engage with your spouse, even if it produces conflict. At least, your spouse will get to know where you stand on the issue at hand.

Contrary to popular opinion, I really believe that some conflict is good for your marriage – if you know how to grow from it. Conflict is simply an opportunity to understand your partner better. It can be the door to your spouse's heart and mind.

Decide not to take conflict too personally, but to understand that it opens the door timely negotiation and necessary compromise. No relationship can really be strong without a measure of conflict. In short, it is not usually the conflict that is the problem; it is how you deal with it and what you learn about yourself and your spouse in the process.

I have been married for over 27 years, and have had hundreds of disagreements, quarrels, clashes, heated verbal arguments and conflicts with my wife; but I can honestly say that the process of resolving them have helped to knit us together like nothing else can. We are, by far, more in-love and more connected today than we've ever been. And, if I had the opportunity to do it all over again, I wouldn't have it any other way.

Stone-walling is insulting and counter-productive. It is annoying and outright irritating. If you want to build a rock solid marriage that would give you the relationship of your dreams, get rid of the habit of stone-walling.

Conclusion

Finally, if you'd take the care to avoid these ten 'relationship killers' in your marriage, you would be well on your way to building the kind of marriage that would inspire and encourage generations to come.

If you are a child of God, it is your right to have a great marriage because your Daddy instituted marriage and gave you a partner to enjoy it with. Draw on God's grace today and go for gold.

You've got what it takes!

Other Books by the Author

How to Build a Rock Solid Marriage – Choices That Will Give You the Marriage of Your Dreams

Stress No More – 20 Healthy Ways To Reduce Stress, Anxiety & Worry.
Maximising Your Season of Singleness – Using Your Season of Singleness to Prepare for Marriage

Keeping God At The Centre Of Your Marriage – Simple Ways To Keep God At The Centre Of Your Relationship

How to Rescue Your Marriage from Breaking Up – Avoiding the Ten Major Relationship Killers

Ten Keys to Effective Communication in Marriage

Find Your Life Partner God's Way – And Say Goodbye To Dating

21 Crucial Things They Don't Teach Young People About Sex

Seven Tools Your Children Should Not Leave Home Without – Equipping Your Children to Excel

Understand Your Marriage Vows - What the Marriage Vows Mean and How to Honour Them

Why God Wants You & Your Family in a Life-giving Church – 12 Reasons to Get Involved in a Great Local Church in Your Area

Why Can't We Talk About It? - 4 Practical Steps to Help Reduce Misunderstandings During Conversations by Shola Peters

How to Find a Life-giving Church – You Can Thrive in

All books are available at **www.amazon.com www.amazon.co.uk, www.smashwords.com, www.rocksolidmarriages.com**

******

Final Word from the Author

Thank you again for getting this book. I intentionally made it light hearted and concise because I don't like reading fat, chunky, padded books either. If you enjoyed this book (and I certainly hope you did), I would appreciate it if you would **rate** it fairly and **post** a short review on **Amazon.com** or **Amazon.co.uk or ibooks,** for other readers. You would certainly be helping other readers who might need some timely advice or encouragement in their marriage, relationships, or family life.

Thank you very much!